£5

D0297179

An Introduction to

Illuminated Manuscripts

COVER ILLUSTRATION: see plate 5

I

Italian (Bologna); *c.* 1500.
Book of Hours (Use of Rome), known as the Bentivoglio Hours. *Antiqua tonda* script in Latin.
21 × 15.5 cm. 112ff.22 pictorial initials.
Rectangular borders filled with Renaissance ornament. The manuscript is unsigned but the scribe was probably Pierantonio Sallando who worked mainly in Bologna from 1489 onwards; he appears to have been still living in 1540. f.1r. Opening page with the coat-of-arms of Giovanni II Bentivoglio (1443-1508), ruler of Bologna. (For this manuscript see Wardrop (James), 'Pierantonio Sallando and Givolamo Pagliarolo, scribes to Giovanni II of Bentivoglio', in *Signature*, N.S., vol 2: 4-30 (1946).)
Reid M.S.64.

An Introduction to

Illuminated Manuscripts

John Harthan

Former Keeper of the Library
Victoria and Albert Museum

LONDON: HER MAJESTY'S STATIONERY OFFICE

Series editor Julian Berry
Designed by HMSO Graphic Design
Printed in England for Her Majesty's Stationery Office

ISBN 0 11 290396 7
Dd 696421 C65

ACKNOWLEDGEMENTS

In compiling this anthology of the illuminated manuscripts in the V & A
Museum I wish to acknowledge with much gratitude help received from
Dr Michael Kauffmann (Keeper of the Department of Prints and Drawings),
Mr Ronald Lightbown (Keeper of the Library) and Dr Christopher de
Hamel (Director in charge of Medieval Manuscripts at Sotheby's), all of
whom read my draft and made valuable suggestions and corrections. To
Mr John Fuller, Mr Robert Howell (Library) and Mr Julian Litten
(Department of Prints and Drawings) I am indebted for assistance in
obtaining photographs and colour transparencies. A few sentences in my
Introduction are based on passages in two earlier works of mine—*Books of
Hours* (Thames and Hudson, 1977), and *The History of the Illustrated Book*,
chapter one (Thames and Hudson, 1981).

John Harthan
November 1981

Detached leaves and cuttings of illuminated manuscripts are kept in the
Department of Prints and Drawings and complete manuscripts in the
Library of the V & A. All plates of manuscripts not in the Library have their
location described in the caption.

HER MAJESTY'S STATIONERY OFFICE

Government Bookshops

49 High Holborn, LondonWC1V 6HB
13a Castle Street, Edinburgh EH2 3AR
Brazennose Street, Manchester M60 8AS
Southey House, Wine Street, Bristol BS1 2BQ
258 Broad Street, Birmingham B1 2HE
80 Chichester Street, Belfast BT1 4JY

Government Publications are also available through booksellers

The full range of Museum publications is displayed and sold at
The Victoria & Albert Museum, South Kensington, London SW7 2RL

Introduction

The importance of manuscript illumination in the history of medieval painting is now generally realised. Tucked away safely between the closed pages of books for several centuries and protected from exposure to light, miniatures have retained a freshness of colouring that no other form of medieval art can emulate. The few wall paintings which have survived from the period are usually in fragmentary, over-restored condition. Easel or panel paintings are not found in any number until the fourteenth century. Mosaic is perhaps the only medium which approaches book illumination in its resistance to time but it was an art form practised mainly in the early centuries of the Middle Ages whereas book illumination has a continuous history and development extending over more than a thousand years. In illuminated manuscripts are found some of the earliest surviving attempts at landscape painting, representation of perspective and incipient realism. Despite the ravages of time they still exist in vast numbers, and new, superlative examples continue to emerge from obscurity to dazzle the sale rooms.

The Anatomy of Illumination

Illumination is the art of decorating books with colours and metals, usually gold, occasionally silver, a form of ornamentation chiefly practised during medieval times when all books were written by hand. The term derives from the Latin verb *illuminare* (Middle English *enluminen*) meaning to 'brighten' or 'light up'. Pictures and various forms of embellishment painted in bright colours heightened by gold produced a sparkling effect which literally lighted up the vellum pages on which the text was written. It is important to bear in mind that illumination comprises both illustration of a text in the strict sense, and its decoration or embellishment about which more will be said.

Since the majority of medieval illuminated manuscripts were religious in content, illumination also shed light, in a more metaphorical sense, on the doctrine and teaching of the Church. It added something to the text, a pictorial elucidation of the book's message, enhanced by decorative elements, in a manner similar to the modern visual aid. Hence the close association of manuscript illumination with the Church, which in the Middle Ages was all pervasive and in some periods more powerful than the secular state.

In the early centuries book production was exclusively monastic. Manuscripts, both illuminated and plain, originated in the scriptoria attached to great monasteries such as Monte Cassino, St Martin de Tours, Echternach, Winchester and St Albans. The names of a few individual monks who specialised in book production have survived, but professional scribes are known to have been employed in monasteries as early as the first decades of the twelfth century (according to the Abingdon Chronicle, Rolls Ser. 1858, ii, p.289). There is also evidence that much of the illumination and decoration of manuscripts was done by itinerant lay artists who travelled from one monastery to another though it is difficult to establish the precise period when this practice became common. The popular image of monks toiling devotedly over illuminated missals thus needs considerable qualification.

From the thirteenth century onwards book production and illumination became progressively secularised and independent of monastic control. This transition was signalled by the appearance of lay workshops in the larger towns where scribes and illuminators organised themselves into craftsmens' guilds. The increasing influence of the universities and of scholastic manuscript production were further factors in the secularisation of manuscript illumination. Literacy was no longer confined to the clergy. A prosperous, urban, literate middle class came into being with a taste for secular literature.

The Elements in Illumination

Manuscript illumination is essentially a composite art form in which several elements are brought together to illustrate and embellish a text. The basic elements are the script, the initial, the miniature and the border. Many scripts were evolved during the Middle Ages but in the thirteenth to the sixteenth centuries, to which period belong most of the examples of illumination here reproduced, two main categories may be distinguished: the angular gothic or *textura* scripts found north of the Alps, and the more rounded *rotunda* scripts developed in Italy by the scribes in the Papal chancellery and by humanist scholars; to these must be added the humanistic cursive hand known as italic.

Initials were either written in ink by the scribe, frequently with calligraphic pen flourishes, or painted in colour by the illuminator (in the early centuries of the Middle Ages it is thought that the same individual often did both). When painted, the initial may be either purely decorative (with a foliage or strapwork design), or pictorial with a little illustration inside the letter shape. These were known in medieval times as *ystoires* or *histoires*, hence the modern term 'historiated initial'. The current use of the expression 'pictorial initial' is perhaps to be welcomed for its greater clarity of meaning.

Miniatures are illustrations to the text in the broadest sense. They usually include figures, animals and other objects relevant to the text, and may be of any size ranging from the little scenes found in historiated initials to full-page pictures unaccompanied by text. The word is derived from *minium*, the red pigment (lead oxide) used by the scribe to rubricate, *i.e.* emphasise, initial letters. *Miniare* meant to write or paint in vermilion and the artist who did so was the miniator. Unlike the portrait miniatures of Tudor and Stuart times, the miniatures in manuscripts were not isolated pictures but a sequence of illustrations only to be fully understood by reference to the text which they accompany. In certain types of manuscripts, especially liturgical books, a fixed scheme of illustration and a standardised iconography were evolved.

Borders, the fourth element in illumination, may be of several kinds. The most basic is the simple rectangular frame surrounding a miniature which separates it from the text. This form was enlarged in manuscripts of the Winchester school (tenth–eleventh centuries) and in manuscripts of the Ottonian and Romanesque periods into wide panels filled with a variety of closely packed foliage ornament among which appear clambering beasts and human figures [plate 4]. In the later Gothic period another type of border developed from the extension of the initial into the margins of the page. These 'bar-borders', as they are sometimes called, were at first somewhat angular and crude [plate 10] but later sprouted into delicate and prolific clusters of foliage, usually ivy-leaf or acanthus, completely filling the margins [plate 12].

The border was the favourite habitat of the miscellaneous cast of drolleries which is such an engaging feature of manuscript illumination. These grotesque creatures, monsters, animals in human guise, baboons or monkeys (known as *babewynnes*), birds, insects, musicians and acrobats are very common in the Psalters and Books of Hours which well-to-do people took to church or castle chapel for personal devotions. Playful secular imagery of this kind may seem out of place in such books, and it is curious that it is found much less frequently in secular texts where it might be thought more appropriately to belong. But this reaction misinterprets the medieval approach to life. Although Christian belief was seldom doubted, the mingling of profane and religious motifs in art was accepted with little question. The juxtaposition of unrelated themes in books nominally made for devotion diverted their owners from the tedium of long church services while at the same time giving scope for the artist's fantasy.

Codicology

The making of an illuminated manuscript was a complex, expensive process in which a number of craftsmen might be involved. To establish the order in which the component parts were completed, and their mutual relationship, the science of codicology has been developed. By this term is meant the systematic analysis of all aspects of a manuscript considered as a whole: size and format, the arrangement of the leaves of vellum in groupings known as quires or gatherings, the pricking and ruling of the lines on which the text was subsequently written [plate 16], the type of script used, the colour and quality of the ink, identification of the text, its embellishment by painted initials, borders and line-endings (*versets*), its illustration by miniatures, with an analysis of their technique and iconography, and finally, the binding, especially of the original one. To these physical aspects are added historical data, where known, concerning the manuscript's provenance, first or early owner, rebinding and subsequent history and changes of ownership until it reached its present location.

The basic unit of a manuscript is always a leaf of vellum folded so that it forms a double leaf or *bifolium* which can be stitched along the fold and joined to other similar leaves. Unlike printed books, manuscripts were seldom originally paginated. Instead, enumeration of the leaves is by folio numbers, the right and left sides of each folio being known as the recto and verso. The sequence of the *bifolia* and their arrangement in quires is known as collation. Since scribes often made mistakes in copying texts, extra leaves had sometimes to be added, or removed, before a book was ready for binding. Leaves with painted miniatures were also often inserted in manuscripts after the collation had been completed. The Utrecht Book of Hours *c.*1440 is an example [plate 17]. The student of illumination needs to know something about codicology and collation in order to appreciate the unique nature of each manuscript. No two are exactly alike. Each has a personal history as well as a physical identity which can only be fully understood if its component parts and historical aspects are studied as a whole.

Workshop Procedures

Our knowledge of workshop procedures and of how manuscripts were produced is still very incomplete. Model or pattern books were certainly used as a few surviving examples demonstrate. Paris was the centre of manuscript illumination in the later Middle Ages; a fact recorded by Dante in a famous and much quoted passage in the *Divine Comedy*. The lay workshops specialising in the production of illuminated manuscripts appear to have been directed by a *maître d'atelier* with a supporting team of craftsmen. But it is now thought that booksellers (or stationers as they were more often called, from having a station or shop) also played an important role in masterminding the operation, calling in illuminators when required. An important example is the fifteenth century Florentine bookseller Vespasiano da Bisticci who enjoyed the patronage of many collectors of fine manuscripts but was not himself an artist.

It is probable that the text was written first by one or more scribes with spaces left blank for initials and miniatures. The unbound sheets were then passed to the illuminator who added coloured borders and initials. Finally came the master craftsman who painted the *histoires* or miniatures. He might be, but was not necessarily, the *maître d'atelier*. The design was first drawn in outline and, if burnished gold was to be used, a covering of sized clay was applied to the vellum within the design. Gold leaf was then laid on with an adhesive and burnished with an agate stone or a dog's tooth. Another method, much used in the fifteenth century, was to apply the gold in powdered liquid form which produced a matt, less glittering, effect of yellow ochre. The last stage was the application of colour, usually red and blue, but also yellow, green and pink.

The result was a simultaneous presentation of text, script, decoration and illustration, in which the stress laid on illustration and decoration varied in different periods. An illuminated manuscript was usually a collective enterprise, seldom the work of one man. In a busy workshop there would be several craftsmen, scribes and artists, each specialising in one branch of book production: preparation of the vellum leaves, transcription of the text, painting of initials, borders and miniatures, and application and burnishing of gold leaf.

In the fourteenth and fifteenth centuries the number of miniature painters steadily increased. Some are known by name and can be associated from documentary evidence with specific manuscripts. But many remain anonymous, known only by recognisable stylistic peculiarities found in widely distributed manuscripts. In exasperating contrast, there are many illuminators mentioned by name in documents who cannot now be linked with any surviving manuscripts. A baffling uncertainty still shrouds the identity of some of the finest book painters who have perforce been named after their patrons. The Boucicaut, Bedford and Rohan Masters, to cite only three outstanding early fifteenth century French artists, come into this category.

Which Books Were Illuminated?

Religious Texts

When studying manuscript illumination it is useful to know something about the types of books which received this de luxe treatment. They divide into two basic groups: religious and secular. The former mainly comprise liturgical texts used in church services or private devotions, such as Books of Hours; but one must not forget the writings of the great theologians, St Augustine, Duns Scotus, St Thomas Aquinas, Gerson, Anselm of Canterbury and many more. These were not often illustrated or elaborately illuminated (though some sumptuous examples exist), and since no specimens are to be found in the Museum collections religious books are here almost entirely confined to the liturgical texts.

In choice of subject the Bible has always offered artists a wide choice—vivid Old Testament scenes, portraits of Prophets and Evangelists, and much else. But it was chiefly Bibles made for ceremonial use, such as the famous Winchester Bible, made *c*.1150-80 (still in the Winchester Cathedral Library) which were elaborately illuminated and decorated; not the smaller Bibles which friars and others carried around for teaching purposes. As a vehicle for illumination the Psalter was as important, perhaps more so, as the Bible since it formed the kernel for both monastic and private devotion. It was preceded by a Calendar, essential for establishing the days when the feasts of the Church and anniversaries of the saints were to be celebrated. The illustrations of the zodiacal signs and occupations or labours of the months found in the Calendars of Psalters, other liturgical books and in Books of Hours form a pictorial sequence of great diversity and interest in manuscript illumination [plate 16].

Between the Calendar and the Psalter proper, a series of miniatures unrelated to the text was often inserted. These usually comprised scenes from the Old and New Testaments. An important English Romanesque example, dating from *c*.1140, is reproduced in plate 7. In only the grandest Psalters was each of the 150 Psalms separately illustrated. The more usual practice was to limit illustrations either to the eight sections into which the Psalter was divided for weekly recital in monastic churches ('liturgical Psalters'), or to numbers 1, 51 and 101, which divided the Psalter into three equal parts. The latter arrangement is commonly found in Psalters made for royalty, wealthy ecclesiastics and feudal magnates and their wives, for whom they served as personal prayerbooks until they were superseded in the fourteenth century by the smaller and more popular Books of Hours. In nearly all Psalters the first psalm beginning with the words 'Beatus Vir' is embellished with a fine decorative initial or with a miniature of King David, the reputed author, playing his harp.

Until the twelfth century the most important liturgical book of the Church was the Sacramentary since it contained the Canon of the Mass but not the Epistles, Gospels and other parts of this central rite, for the text of which separate volumes were provided. Magnificent illuminated Sacramentaries were made in Carolingian times but the book was gradually replaced by the more comprehensive Missal into which all of the Latin texts necessary for the celebration of the Mass throughout the year were gathered together in one volume. In Missals large or full-page miniatures are usually found only at the Preface ('Sursum Corda') and Canon ('Te igitur'). The subject of the first was usually a priest at an altar, of the second Christ in Majesty or the Crucifixion [plates 6 & 9]. Elaborately decorated Missals were seldom produced. The example from the Abbey of St Denis is a rare and resplendent example [plate 11].

The Breviary, like the Missal, is a composite volume containing not only the Psalter but all the other texts, prayers, hymns and antiphons needed for the Divine Office, or daily service, recited by monks and clerics throughout the Church's year. It was not always illustrated, but sumptuous examples illustrated with scenes from Bible history or the lives of the saints were sometimes made.

Finally, we come to the large choir books (Antiphoners and Graduals) which contained the musical chants used in church services. These *libri corali* were placed on lecterns where they could be seen by a group of choristers. In the fourteenth and fifteenth centuries magnificent examples were produced in Italy. Fewer examples have survived from northern countries, perhaps because of destruction at the time of the Reformation. Choir books have been peculiarly liable to mutilation. During the Napoleonic invasions of Italy many monastic libraries were pillaged, their beautiful choir books stolen and vandalised. However, the books were too big to be all looted. The large initials were cut out and separated from the musical notation which was often thrown away.

The most popular religious book of the late medieval period, the best-seller of its time, was the Book of Hours. It originated as an appendix to the Psalter but in the thirteenth century became detached and assumed an independent life as the favourite prayerbook of the laity. An enormous number were produced: decorated with every degree of luxury from modest, mass-produced examples to specially commissioned individual copies of great splendour destined for royalty, prelates and high-born ladies.

Secular Texts

But what of secular illumination? Simultaneously with the religious books appeared vernacular texts handsomely illuminated and widely circulated among the rich and powerful ruling classes and the prosperous urban bourgeoisie. The texts most often illustrated and decorated can be grouped into broad categories. First were chivalrous histories, chronicles, romances and epic poems dealing with subjects like the Trojan War, Alexander the Great, King Arthur, Charlemagne and his paladins (the Chanson de Roland), which had a strong romantic appeal for a feudal society. Travels in far-off exotic countries formed another group of popular books. A third group comprised scientific works such as medical treatises, herbals, hunting books and encyclopedias. Of the latter the most important was the *De proprietatibus rerum* written *c.*1220 by Bartholomew the Englishman. It was translated into most of the vernacular languages, copiously illustrated, and remained the basic reference book on natural history until Shakespeare's time.

Last, but still one of the most important categories of secular illumination, were the Greek and Roman classics which survived from antiquity or had been rediscovered at the time of the Renaissance. The comedies of Terence had always been popular on account of the excellence of his Latin, a model for clerics and schoolboys alike, and the *Psychomachia*, or the Battle of the Virtues and Vices, by Prudentius (died *c.*410), the contemporary of Ss Jerome, Augustine and Ambrose, was illustrated both in the West and in the Byzantine East. Virgil had been read throughout the Middle Ages and two very early illustrated codices, dating from the fifth century, survive in the Vatican Library. A marked revival of interest in Virgil at the turn of the fifteenth century was responsible for such famous illustrated and decorated manuscripts as the Urbino Codex (British Library) and the Siena Codex (Vatican Library). In Italy a number of other classical authors were profusely illustrated including Pliny [plate 24] as well as native writers such as Boccaccio and Petrarch [plate 26]. But, speaking generally, the humanist scholars preferred the decoration of classical texts to be limited to the first or title-page of their manuscripts. Many of the decorated literary and classical manuscripts came from the flourishing Florentine workshop organised by the publisher Vespasiano da Bisticci.

Historical Development

The evolution in the first five centuries AD of the codex or bound book as we know it today, as distinct from papyrus rolls or *rotuli*, was an event as important in the history of book production as the invention of printing in the fifteenth century. Sheets of vellum or parchment, prepared from animal skins, provided more space for writing and pictures and were more durable than the fragile rolls made from the Egyptian papyrus plant. When bound together, vellum leaves formed substantial volumes in which complete texts could be assembled and illustrated. A few codices of the works of Virgil and Homer survive from late Roman times. The classical, pagan style of painting found in these manuscripts was taken over and adapted to Christian purposes in the fourth century AD after the Emperor Constantine had made Christianity the official religion of the Empire. From early days the codex was closely associated with the Christian Church and played an important role in spreading its doctrines and liturgy. The triumph of the new book form was signalled by Constantine's order for fifty copies of the Scriptures, written on parchment codices, to be made for the churches of his new capital in the East, the old Byzantium re-named Constantinople after its founder.

Many of the forms and pictorial conventions of classical manuscripts were preserved in the work of Byzantine book artists in Constantinople and other centres of the East Roman Empire. There the classical tradition came under Syrian and other near-Eastern influences and underwent considerable stylistic development before being re-disseminated in Europe where Byzantine models became an important ingredient in Carolingian and Ottonian art and illumination [plate 3].

Somewhat apart from the classical tradition but preserving certain Hellenistic motifs was the Coptic art of the Christian communities in Egypt. The early manuscripts received no embellishment but from the eighth century onwards zoomorphic decoration appeared in the margins, doves pecking at, or holding fragments of, foliage in their beaks are a common feature [plate 2].

But medieval manuscript illumination was more than a survivor of the classical world; it emerged from the fusion of two entirely different cultural streams, the classical tradition of late antiquity,

2
Egyptian; 8-11th centuries. Fragments from Coptic manuscripts, found at Akhmin (Panopolis), Upper Egypt. *Presented by Mrs Henry Wallis.* Dept. of Prints & Drawings. E6337-8-1910.

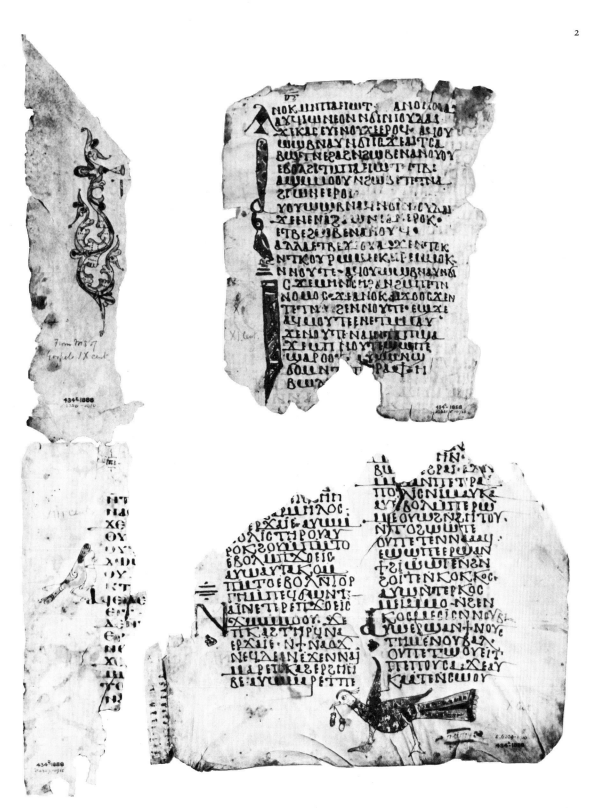

already mentioned, and the northern or 'Insular' style of the barbaric tribes which invaded the Roman Empire in the fourth and fifth centuries AD. The earliest independent schools of book-painting in the West appeared in Merovingian Gaul, Visigothic Spain, Celtic Ireland and Anglo-Saxon Northumbria. Monasticism in Ireland may have been introduced as early as the fifth century by monks who possibly had visited Egypt. More certain is the transmission of the Insular, formerly called Celtic or Hiberno-Saxon, style of book decoration to Scotland and Northumbria. Irish missionaries, led by St Columba, founded the monastery on Iona, an islet off the larger island of Mull in the west of Scotland, in 563. Iona, in its turn, established the monastery of Lindisfarne off the Northumbrian coast in 635.

The precise Irish and English (Northumbrian) contributions to the Insular style of the seventh and eighth centuries is a complex question which has not yet been fully resolved. Less controversial is the fact that Insular book decoration drew heavily on the repertoire of abstract barbaric ornament—ribbon interlacings, spiral patterns, stylised biting beasts—a style in total contrast to the classical tradition with its emphasis on the human figure. The reconciliation with, and fusion of, such diverse traditions was a stupendous achievement by medieval book artists.

With the Insular school of illumination are associated some of the most celebrated of illuminated manuscripts—the Book of Durrow, c.657-700 (Dublin, Trinity College Library, MS. A.4.5 (57), the Lindisfarne Gospels, c.690 (London, British Library, Cotton MS. Nero D. IV) and the Book of Kells, c.800 or later in the early ninth century (Dublin, Trinity College Library, MS. A.1.6). But the beginning of a continuous tradition of manuscript illumination in Europe dates only from the rise of the Carolingian Empire in the late eighth century and the coronation in Rome in the year 800 of Charlemagne as head of a newly constituted Holy Roman Germanic Empire.

Examples of Carolingian and Ottonian illumination are unfortunately lacking in the V&A collections but from the twelfth century onwards there are sufficient examples to illustrate the principal phases in the development of Romanesque and Gothic manuscript illumination. In Romanesque illumination the initial became the central feature. Often of large size, initials were decorated with interlacing foliage scrolls inhabited by biting beasts, birds and climbing human figures. The letter shape itself is often formed of a writhing beast with the foliage relegated to a rectangular panel background as in the Rhenish or Mosan example from a twelfth-century choir book reproduced in plate 4: also German is the slightly later initial Q from a Cistercian Psalter. Here the foliage is subservient to the emphatic interlacing strapwork issuing from the mouth of the isolated wyvern-like creature below, the latter forming the tail of the initial letter [plate 5].

16

3
Byzantine; 12th century.
Detached leaf from a Book of the Gospels.
30.5 × 20 cm.
St Mark writing on a scroll, with writing implements
on the table below.
Dept. of Prints & Drawings.
8980 E.

4
Rhenish or Mosan; second half of 12th century.
Detached leaf from a Gradual.
30.4 × 20.5 cm.
Initial S composed of a dragon and interlacing scrolls.
Dept. of Prints & Drawings.
244.1 (MS. 15).

5
German; *c*.1260.
Psalter (with Canticles), Calendar and fragment of the
Office of the Dead from an unidentified Cistercian
monastery. Gothic script in Latin.
17.9 × 13.5 cm. 180ff. 10 large illuminated initials,
numerous small decorative initials at the beginning of
individual psalms.
f.44 Initial Q ('Quid gloriaris in ora malicia') divided
from the bottom of the page by a green frame. The
large dragon-wyvern with twisted tail beneath forms
the tail of the initial.
MS. L.23.iii.1870.

6
English; *c*.1200.
Missal from Lesnes Abbey. Gothic script in Latin.
33 × 24 cm. 196ff. 41 pictorial or decorative initials.
Lesnes Abbey was a monastery of the Austin Canons
founded at Erith, Kent, by Richard de Lucy, Grand
Justiciar of England, who retired and died there in
1179. The fishes ('luces' or pike) which appear
prominently in the stems of the initials allude to the
canting arms of the Lucy family (three gold luces on
a red field). The Lesnes Missal is liturgically important
as one of the earliest English manuscripts to combine
in one volume the texts needed for saying Mass
throughout the year.
f.76. Canon of the Mass ('Sursum corda'). Initial P
with a priest at the altar and the Paschal Lamb in a
medallion below.
Presented by Sir Otto Beit.
MS. L.304-1916.

English examples of Romanesque illumination are represented by the Lesnes Missal [plate 6], one of the earliest known English missals, and the superlative detached leaf of New Testament scenes from the Psalter already mentioned [plate 7]. The Museum leaf is one of four to survive from what once must have been a magnificent manuscript; together they constitute the largest New Testament cycle produced in England in the twelfth century.

The transition from the late Romanesque to the early Gothic style is seen in an initial A from an Antiphoner made c.1290 for the Abbey of Beaupré, a Cistercian house near Grammont, showing a pope and a bishop with kneeling Cistercian monks beside them [plate 8].

The Gothic style first appeared in the architecture of the *Ile de France* in the late twelfth century. Gothic architectural motifs, canopies and pointed niches, soon found their way into manuscript illumination although in the early Gothic period miniatures and pictorial initials usually still show gold backgrounds; diapered backgrounds of contrasting colours and the first attempts at landscape settings came later. In Gothic illumination the decorative and illustrative elements become fused more successfully than in any other period. Whereas in earlier times decoration had often taken precedence over illustration, book painters now achieved a masterly balance with the miniature becoming one of the most important expressions of the art of the High Gothic.

The page from a Book of Hours made c.1300 for use in the diocese of Rheims is a vigorous example of the early Gothic style with incipient bar-borders extending from the pictorial initial and supporting grotesque creatures [plate 10]. This manuscript provides an introduction to the mature Gothic style seen in the Missal from the Abbey of St Denis, one of the finest manuscripts in the V & A collection [plate 11].

The St Denis Missal, together with a companion Breviary (Oxford, Bodleian Library, MS. Canon. Liturg. 192) also made for use in the royal abbey of St Denis, shows the developed Gothic style in the refined and delicate form in which it appears in contemporary small-scale ivory carvings and diptychs. The miniatures are immediately recognisable as the work of a master artist with a feeling for space not found before in manuscript illumination. The borders are already sprouting with ivy-leaf tendrils, though not yet with the profusion of the later Gothic style, among which appear birds and insects observed with a freshness of eye suggesting close observation from nature.

The artist responsible for this new mood in French illumination was Jean Pucelle, one of the first illuminators to be known both by name and documented works; he was the most important figure in Parisian book painting in the fourteenth century. His miniatures show familiarity with Florentine and Sienese *trecento* painting. He is thought to have visited Italy in the early 1320s, or just possibly

7
English; *c*.1140.
Detached leaf from a Psalter. Canterbury (?), Christ
Church Abbey.
40 × 30 cm.
Four leaves from this large and once magnificent
Psalter are known, two in the Pierpont Morgan
Library, New York, one in the British Library, and
one in the V &A. The latter is painted on both sides
with 24 New Testament scenes from the life of Christ.
Each side contains twelve compartments, some
divided. (For this leaf see Kauffmann C.M.,
Romanesque Manuscripts, 1066–1190, no. 66).
Dept. of Prints & Drawings. MS. 661.

8
Flemish; early 13th century.
Cutting from an Antiphoner made for Beaupré, a
Cistercian abbey near Grammont.
30.5 × 17 cm. Initial A with Pope, Bishop and two
kneeling Cistercian monks.
Dept. of Prints & Drawings.
7940.

8

9

9
Italian (probably Venice); *c*.1300.
Missal (Roman). Rotunda script in Latin.
18.5 × 13 cm. 101ff. 1 miniature on f.27 (of the
Crucifixion) at the Canon of the Mass, with highly
burnished and raised gold ground.
The miniature is surrounded by a double border of
geometrical patterning but the page was never
completed by the insertion of the opening words of
the Canon of the Mass ('Te igitur') in the blank space
beneath the miniature. This is the reverse of the usual
order in manuscript production when the text was
written first.
Reid MS. 65.

10
French; c.1300.
Book of Hours (Use of Rheims), once owned by
John Ruskin. *Textura* script in Latin.
13.5 × 10.5 cm. 228ff. 9 full-page miniatures on gold
grounds, 33 pictorial initials, and stiff bar borders
with foliage, grotesques and monsters.
f.19v. The Nativity.
Reid MS. 83.

11
French (Paris), School of Jean Pucelle; c.1350.
Missal of Saint-Denis Abbey, Paris. *Textura* script in
Latin.
23.5 × 17 cm. 426ff. 19 pictorial initials and small
miniatures in rectangular frames partly painted in
grisaille. 10 smaller grisaille paintings without frames.
f.261. Pictorial initial O at the Feast of St Denis, with
a hunting scene and two grisaille paintings at the
bottom of the page. All three miniatures depict
episodes in St Denis's miraculous intervention in the
affairs of the French royal family: 1) a stag, pursued
by Dagobert, son of King Clotaire, takes refuge in a
church where the bodies of the martyred saint and his
companions are kept; dogs and huntsmen are
powerless to enter; 2) St Denis and his companions
appear to Dagobert in a dream as he sleeps in the
church after quarreling with his father; 3) King
Clotaire and his followers go in search of Dagobert,
find him and are reconciled. In the initial O at the top
of the page the placing of the arch of the church
across the letter shape gives a sense of spatial recession
new in miniature painting.
MS.L.1346-1891.

may have had Italian antecedents himself; it has been suggested, as a hypothesis, that his unusual name could be a French version of the Italian *puccelli* (*Bulletin of the Metropolitan Museum*, New York, February 1971).

As Jean Pucelle his name occurs in contemporary documents and many years afer his death in 1334 he was remembered in the will of Queen Jeanne d'Evreux (d.1371), widow of Charles IV, in which she bequeathed to the reigning King Charles V her exquisite Book of Hours (now in the Cloisters Museum, New York) which she specifically states to have been illuminated by Pucelle. After his death the Pucelle style, and probably workshop, continued to dominate Parisian illumination for the rest of the century. François Avril attributes the Saint-Denis Missal to the illuminator who executed a copy of Guillaume de Machaut's *Le remède de fortune* (Paris, Bibl. Nat. 1586). The Missal is none-the-less a choice example of the Pucelle style; from entries and obits in the Calendar of deceased Kings and Abbots of Saint-Denis it can be dated with great probability to the year 1350.

Parisian illumination reached its zenith in the early fifteenth century. This was in part due to court patronage on the grandest scale which attracted a number of superlative artists to the capital. Prominent among these were the three Limbourg brothers who came from Guelders to work for Jean, Duke of Berry (d.1416), brother of King Charles V. He was one of the greatest patrons and connoisseurs of any time, amassing enormous collections of precious metalwork and jewellery, as well as tapestries and books, in his various castles. Nearly all his treasures have long since vanished, but the *Très Riches Heures*, the most famous of Books of Hours, still survives in the Musée Condé at Chantilly. Renowned for its Calendar illustrations, it proved to be the swansong of the Limbourg brothers, all of whom died suddenly in the same year as their patron leaving their finest manuscript unfinished.

Equally outstanding was the Boucicaut Master, so-called from the Book of Hours he illuminated for Jean Le Meingre, Maréchal de Boucicaut, his patron who died in England in 1421 after being taken prisoner at the Battle of Agincourt (1415). The manuscript is now in the Musée Jacquemart-André, Paris. The Boucicaut Master and the Limbourg brothers, in their treatment of landscape, perspective, light and colour, added a new dimension to manuscript illumination. At the same time their work embodies the spirit of the courtly Gothic International Style of painting in its most rarified form. A blending of features taken from French, Flemish, Sienese, Lombard and Bohemian art, the International Style was primarily a northern manifestation of the idealised, stylised yet at the same time realistic (in its observation of nature, for example) self-image projected by feudal society and the cosmopolitan courts of the late Middle Ages.

Besides being a pioneering artist in his own right, the Boucicaut Master was also the director of a busy workshop in Paris. Here many assistants must have been employed producing competent manuscripts which disseminated and diluted the Master's style. The Boucicaut workshop also had connections with other workshops, but how this collaboration was arranged is unknown. The late Professor Millard Meiss, who studied the work of the Boucicaut Master in great detail, has listed dozens of manuscripts connected with the Boucicaut workshop in one way or another, and even speaks of the 'Boucicaut Associates'. The Boucicaut manuscript in the Museum collections belongs to the latter. It is a workshop product which nonetheless conveys the authentic Boucicaut style [plate 12].

A third artist to be mentioned in the same breath as the Boucicaut Master and the Limbourg brothers is the Rohan Master. He is so-named from a Book of Hours owned later in the century by the Rohan family of Brittany, but almost certainly made *c*.1420 for Yolanda of Aragon, Duchess of Anjou, wife of Louis of Anjou, the elder brother of the Duke of Berry, or for a member of her family. The Rohan Master's identity is shrouded even more obscurely than that of the Boucicaut or Bedford Masters. His *Grandes Heures de Rohan* (Paris, Bibliothèque Nationale, ms. lat. 1471) is one of the strangest, most haunting of late medieval Books of Hours. But, in a manner similar to that of the Boucicaut workshop, watered-down versions of the Rohan Master's compelling style are found in lesser manuscripts such as the grubby, much thumbed little example reproduced in plate 14.

In the fifteenth, in contrast to the fourteenth, century, a gradual decline in English illumination set in for reasons which are not very clear. The Wars of the Roses did not begin until the 1450s, and in France, where the political climate was much more disturbed than in England in the first decades of the century, first by the civil war in Paris between the Burgundian and Armagnac factions and then by the renewal of the Hundred Years War, illumination continued to flourish. Henry V's conquest of Normandy, the occupation of Paris by the English, and the Treaty of Troyes (1420) which gave the succession to the French throne to the English king, nevertheless seriously weakened the French capital's supremacy in manuscript illumination. In the 1420s a number of scribes and artists moved north to Rouen, the administrative centre of the Anglo-French monarchy, others went to London. But at least one leading illuminator appears to have remained in Paris. Around 1423 the anonymous Bedford Master produced a superb Book of Hours (London, British Library, Add. MS. 18850) on the occasion of the marriage of John of Lancaster, Duke of Bedford, the Regent of France for the infant Henry VI, to Anne, daughter of the Duke of Burgundy.

In England illumination flourished in the fourteenth century. Fine manuscripts were produced in, or associated with, Peterborough and other East Anglian monasteries during the first half of the century though the 'East Anglian' style is found also in manu-

12

French (Paris); early fifteenth century.
Book of Hours (Use of Paris). *Textura* script in Latin.
22 × 14.5 cm. 188ff. 10 full-page miniatures, nine by
the Boucicaut Master and one by the Egerton Master
who worked together in several manuscripts.
Though their styles are quite distinct it is a curious
fact that no single manuscript by the Egerton Master
is known which does not also contain miniatures by
the Boucicaut Master. Both artists belonged to the
circle working for the Duke of Berry. The Egerton
Master is so-called from his authorship of MS.

Egerton 1070 (a Book of Hours once owned by René
of Anjou) now in the British Library, London. All
the surviving miniatures in the V &A manuscript have
ivy-leaf borders except for the single miniature by the
Egerton Master where the border is composed of
acanthus foliage (plate 13).
f.56v. The Nativity. Mary feels the temperature of the
water poured by a woman into the tub in which the
infant Jesus is about to be washed. The Boucicaut
Master workshop.
Reid MS.4.

13
French (Paris); early fifteenth century.
Book of Hours (Use of Paris).
f.16. St Matthew seated before a writing desk. By the
Egerton Master or his workshop (see plate 12).
Reid MS. 4.

French; second quarter of the fifteenth century.
Book of Hours (Use of Paris) from the Rohan Master workshop. *Textura* script in Latin.
7.5 × 5.5 cm. 217ff. 16 large miniatures, the backgrounds either chequered or of dark blue studded with stars and little gold clouds, the latter typical of the Rohan workshop, as are the horizontal bands of ornament on the dress of the two women.
f.37v. The Visitation.
Reid MS. 5.

scripts produced elsewhere. The Queen Mary Psalter (London, British Library, Royal MS. 2. B. vii), one of the finest examples, was probably made in London. Another notable group of manuscripts associated with the powerful family of Bohun appeared in the 1370s.

It is against this complex historical background that the English Psalter here reproduced [plate 15] should be seen. It is in a vigorous, not very refined, Anglo-French style. The so-called Plantagenet Psalter, executed c.1435-45, contains a medieval coronation scene which may be a conscious allusion to Henry V's coronation as King of France in Paris in 1430, or even a recall of the sumptuous Coronation Book of Charles V made in 1380 (London, British Library, Cotton MS. Tiberius B.viii). The border is characteristically French.

Illumination in the Netherlands has so far received scant mention. No very distinctive style emerged before the fourteenth century but from the early fifteenth century there was a rapid development. Netherlandish illumination was a powerful influence on French book painting (the work of the Limbourg brothers has already been noted) and brought new vigour to the somewhat mannered, post-Boucicaut International Gothic tradition.

Although not politically divided on nationalistic lines in the fifteenth century, it is important to distinguish between the northern provinces (approximately modern Holland), where the centre of manuscript illumination was at Utrecht, and the southern or Flemish provinces (approximately modern Belgium), where a brilliant school of illumination flourished in the cities of Bruges and Ghent.

North Netherlandish illumination displays a zest for the anecdotal incident which anticipates the great Dutch school of painting in the seventeenth century. There was also considerable use of grisaille. In the miniatures painted in this technique c.1440 and inserted in an Utrecht Book of Hours there is a pondered pathos of effect in marked contrast to the elegant style found in grisailles of the courtly Paris school of Pucelle and his successors [plate 17].

Also of North Netherlandish provenance is the so-called Aberdeen Book of Hours, though the most interesting of the three surviving miniatures, an unfinished portrait of Saint Christopher, may have been added after the manuscript reached Scotland [plate 18].

The South Netherlandish school was more sophisticated and became more important in the late fifteenth century. Guillaume Vrelant (d.1481/2) who came to Bruges from Utrecht around 1454, established there a guild of illuminators under the patronage of St John the Baptist. The extent to which he actively participated in producing manuscripts is a matter of some uncertainty. He may have been merely the organiser of the trade in fine manuscripts. But in the decade 1470-80 an innovation of great importance made its appearance in manuscripts of the Ghent-Bruges school. This was the

English; *c.*1435-45.
Psalter (with Sarum calendar),
known as the Plantagenet Psalter.
Textura script in Latin.
28.5 × 19.5 cm. 203ff. Nine large
miniatures with full-page borders
in an Anglo-French style.
f.30 Coronation of David,
represented by an English
coronation. The venerable king
with long white beard, an ideal
type of medieval king, is perhaps
intended to represent Henry VI
(who was still very young in the
period when the manuscript was
written).
Reid MS. 42.

North French (Rouen?); *c.*1480.
Book of Hours (Use of Rouen).
Bastarda script in Latin and
French.
17.5 × 11 cm. 96ff. 14 large
miniatures in text in architectural
frames. 24 smaller miniatures in
Calendar of the zodiacal signs and
occupations of the months.
f.3r. Calendar entry for May. In
lower border a man on a horse
(hawking?) with a woman riding
postillion. In right border the
Gemini sign of a naked man and
woman embracing. The Gemini
sign was one of the few places in
Books of Hours where artists
could portray nudity. The
Calendar is only partly filled
with names of saints in gold,
blue and red, and shows the
system of pricking and ruling
lines on the vellum prior to
writing.
Reid MS. 17.

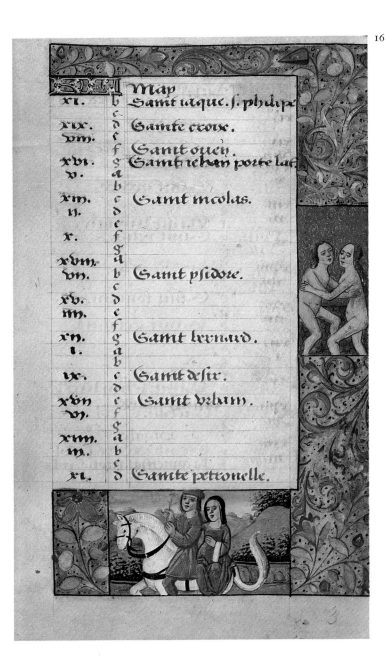

North Netherlandish (Utrecht);
c.1440.
Book of Hours (Use of Utrecht).
Textura script in Dutch.
19 × 13 cm. 180ff. 16 large
miniatures, the figures painted in
grisaille with yellow foregrounds
and blue skies. The absence of
borders and of text on the reverse
side of the miniature suggests
that these were a workshop series
produced independently of the
text into which they are now
bound.
f.83v. Christ before Pilate, with
Pilate's wife looking through the
window.
Reid MS. 32.

18
North Netherlandish (probably Utrecht); mid-15th century.
Book of Hours (Use of Rome), known as the Aberdeen Hours. *Textura* script in Latin.
15 × 10 cm. 99ff.
Three miniatures only remain in this Book of Hours which seems to have reached Scotland at an early date. A long rubric in red has been added on f.96v in the Scots vernacular beginning 'Qwha sa says this orysoun dayly devotly he sal hafe ful remissions of al hys synns et he sal noth de na sodan death'. (Sudden death was a fate much feared by medieval men and women since it gave no time to be shriven and absolved of sins.) Two further prayers and inscriptions record that the book was in the Aberdeen neighbourhood in the

16th and 17th centuries. It is one of the few illuminated devotional manuscripts to have survived the fanaticism of the Scottish Reformation.
f.41v. One of the miniatures later in date than the other two, is an unusual depiction of St Christopher carrying the Christ Child. It is unfinished and may have been added after the manuscript reached Scotland. The absence of borders and the size of the central group (the Christ Child's halo has indeed been cut off by the binder), are interesting but inconclusive indications of the successive processes of manuscript illumination. The miniature was usually the last item to be completed, but this does not appear to have been the case in this particular manuscript.
Reid MS. 53.

use of wide, gold-painted borders filled with large chopped-off heads of naturalistic flowers, often accompanied by birds and insects. This produced an illusionistic or *trompe l'oeil* effect of bringing the border close to the spectator's eye so that it becomes like a window frame through which the miniature is seen as if it were on another plane of vision. This reconciliation of two-dimensional script with three-dimensional painting on the flat surface of the page brought a new lease of life to manuscript illumination which lasted until well into the sixteenth century [plate 19].

The new sense of spatial recession in the miniature was highly developed in the work of the anonymous Master of Mary of Burgundy, the leading artist in the Ghent-Bruges school. It is equally characteristic of Simon Bening (c.1483-1561), one of the last great book painters of the school. His style, if not his hand, is seen in a magnificent though sadly incomplete Book of Hours made in Ghent-Bruges, c.1515. Two exceptional full-page miniatures remain, David in penitence at the Penitential Psalms, and a Funeral Mass before the Office of the Dead with a funeral procession in the full-page border on the facing page [plate 20].

Two Flemish manuscripts of the highest quality and smallest size in the Museum collections are the so-called Simon Marmion Hours and the Hours of Cardinal Marco Sittico Hohenembs. The former, strictly speaking, is Franco-Flemish since the artist Simon Marmion (d.1489), to whose workshop the manuscript has been attributed (see the unpublished doctoral thesis 'Simon Marmion' by Edith W. Hoffman (1958), deposited in the Courtauld Institute, London), directed a workshop in Valenciennes in northern France, though he had connections as well with Bruges. The Hohenembs Hours is in the style of Guillaume Vrelant and may well be a product of his Bruges workshop. These two choice manuscripts illustrate the vogue at the end of the fifteenth century for very small prayerbooks. Examples are known with hooks on the bindings enabling them to be attached to ladies' girdles by means of a chain [plates 21 & 22].

In Italy national styles of illumination developed later than in other countries and lasted longer. Until the thirteenth century illumination was primarily monastic and remained severely Byzantine in character. The Crucifixion miniature in a Missal made c.1300 is a late example. The figure of the drooping Christ (with feet separately nailed) derives from a much earlier formula [plate 9].

Monastic workshops remained important throughout the four-teenth century. A notable example is that of the Camaldolese monastery of S. Maria degli Angeli in Florence which produced a fine series of *libri corali* between 1370 and 1422. A leading figure of this workshop was the monk Don Silvestro Gheraducci (d.1399) who achieved mention by Vasari in his *Lives of the Painters*. A number of initials from a choir book containing half-length figures of prophets or male saints have been identified as his work by Dott. Mirella Levi d'Ancona. They show the transition from an early

19
North Netherlandish (?); *c*.1500.
Book of Hours (Use of Utrecht). *Bastarda* script in
Latin.
13.5 × 9.5 cm. 209ff. Seven large miniatures with
borders of fruit, flowers, birds and insects on matt
gold borders.
The miniatures are in a coarse Ghent-Bruges style and
it is possible that the manuscript was written and
illuminated in the south Netherlands.
f.47v-48. Massacre of the Innocents.
Reid MS. 35.

20

Flemish; *c*.1515-25.
Book of Hours (Use of Rome). *Rotunda* script in
Latin.
18.4 × 13 cm. 64ff.
An incomplete Book of Hours, made in Ghent-Bruges,
possibly by Simon Bening (1483-1561). The Hours of
the Virgin are entirely lacking, but two exceptional
full-page miniatures remain, David in penitence at the
Penitential Psalms (f.2v) and a Funeral Mass (f.21v).
Five smaller miniatures of saints within full-page
borders of flowers, fruits and leaves, insects, birds and
animals.
f.21v-22r. Funeral Mass before the Office of the Dead,
with, on facing page, a funeral procession. The figures
are painted with great naturalism, the man on the
extreme left could be a portrait of a specific individual.
MS. L.39-1981.

21
Franco-Flemish; 1475–81.
Book of Hours (Use of Rome). *Bastarda* script in
Latin by an Italian hand.
11 × 7.5 cm. 250ff. One full-page miniature, 12 other
miniatures in arched frames within full borders
matching those on the facing page of text.
Two artists (or their workshops) contributed to this
tiny Book of Hours: Simon Marmion (*c*.1425–89) who
worked at Valenciennes *c*.1475–89, and Guillaume
Vrelant (d.1482) who had a workshop in Bruges,
where the manuscript may have been completed.
(a) f.15v–16r. Martyrdom of St Catherine (Vrelant
workshop). (b) f.118v–119. Coronation of the Virgin
(Marmion workshop).
Salting Collection no. 1221. MS. L.2384-1910.

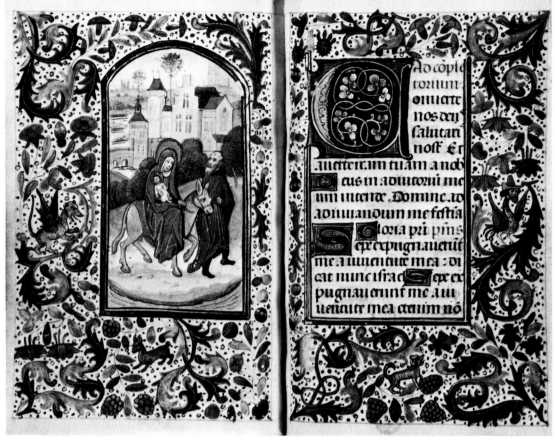

23

22

South Netherlandish (Bruges);
c.1475.
Book of Hours (Use of Rome).
Rotunda script in Latin.
11.5 × 7.5 cm. 263ff. 19
miniatures and nine pictorial
initials.
Probably made in the Vrelant
workshop. Later owned by
Cardinal Marco Sittico
Hohenembs (d.1595), a nephew
of Pope Pius V (1566-72), whose
coat-of-arms appears on f.13v.
f.114v. The Flight into Egypt.
Salting Collection no. 4478.
MS. L.2393-1910.

23

Italian (Florence); late 14th
century.
Cutting from a Choir Book with
initial containing a saint painted
by Don Silvestro Gheraducci
(d.1399), a monk of the
Camaldolese monastery of
S.Maria degli Angeli, Florence.
(For this cutting see Levi
d'Ancona (Mirella), 'Don
Silvestro dei Gheraducci e Il
Maestro delle Canzoni. Due
miniatori trecenteschi della scuola
di S.Maria degli Angeli a
Firenze', in *Rivista d'Arte*,
XXXIII, pp.3-37 (1957).
Dept. of Prints & Drawings.
MS. 975.

Gothic to the developed International Gothic style [plate 23].

With the Renaissance came the most brilliant period in Italian illumination. There was much activity in cities such as Milan, Ferrara and Naples, ruled by a succession of princely patrons who commissioned books in a manner similar to their contemporaries, often relations, at the French court. Important local schools were also established in the city-republics of Venice, Florence and Siena where manuscript illumination was carried out in lay workshops. In Italian Renaissance illumination text and decoration were not so closely integrated as in northern manuscripts, partly on account of the esteem in which fine calligraphy was held by humanist scholars. The classical and literary texts written for or commissioned by individual men of letters (and we are now in a period when secular texts were as frequently illuminated as religious) are characterised by ornamental frontispieces with borders of acanthus foliage, scrolls, putti, sphinxes, trophies of arms, jewellery, candelabra, cornucopiae and other motifs from the repertoire of Renaissance ornament, with a discreet display of heraldry on small shields within laurel wreaths or supported by putti. In the pages following, decoration is often confined to small emblazoned initials, an indication of the humanists' respect for classical texts. A similar decorative ensemble for frontispieces is also found in religious texts such as the Bentivoglio Hours [plate 1 facing title page].

The revival of interest in classical antiquity, one of the most potent influences in Italian Renaissance art, is seen in title-pages and frontispieces painted in direct imitation of Roman funeral monuments and lapidary inscriptions. These were a specialty of the Paduan school of calligraphy and illumination, as seen in the beautiful Petrarch manuscript written by the scribe Bartolomeo Sanvito where the frontispiece faces the opening lines of the first sonnet written in epigraphic capitals [plate 26].

Another type of border was the white-vine interlace which consorted impeccably with the newly developed humanist scripts. It came into fashion in the early fifteenth century when it was erroneously believed to represent the style of illumination practised in antiquity; it was in fact derived from Carolingian and Romanesque manuscripts. The white-vine interlace was used mainly in classical manuscripts, such as the magnificent Pliny reproduced in plate 24. Its appearance in religious, devotional books such as in the Hours of Alfonso of Aragon, Duke of Calabria, is exceptional [plate 25].

A late example of Florentine illumination is the Hours of Eleanora de Toledo which can be be precisely dated to 1540, thanks to the scribe Aloysius who both signed and dated his work. But the identity of the artist who painted the suave Mannerist miniatures is not known [plate 27].

Illumination in Italy was much influenced by contemporary fresco and panel painting. The attempt to reproduce similar

24

Italian (Rome); *c*.1460–70.

Pliny the Elder, *Historia naturalis*. Humanistic *antiqua* script in Latin, probably by Jacopo della Pergola. 42.5 × 30 cm. 526ff. 37 pictorial initials with white-vine interlace borders by the miniaturist Giuliano Amedei who worked for Pope Pius II (Piccolomini). Of special interest in this very large manuscript are the miniatures in Chapter XXXV showing different types of craftsmen at work.

f.485r. Initial M with three small pictures illustrating painting trades: 1) an apprentice grinds colours on a table 2) an artist paints the ceiling of a vaulted hall 3) an artist paints a cassone or marriage chest. Above his head is a shield with the Piccolomini arms. (For this MS. see Whalley (J.I.), Pliny the Elder, Historia Naturalis, V &A Museum, London, 1982.)

MS. A.L.1504-1896.

25

Italian (Naples); *c*.1480.

Book of Hours (Use of Rome), known as the Alfonso of Aragon Hours. *Rotunda* script in Latin. 25.5 × 18.5 cm. 411ff. 13 large miniatures, 14 smaller miniatures in borders, 27 pictorial initials with partial borders.

In this unusually big Book of Hours the large miniatures are framed by white-vine interlace borders, unusual in a religious book, characteristic of Italian 15th century humanist manuscripts. A Neapolitan provenance is indicated by the presence of parrots, among other fauna, in the border decoration. The book formerly belonged to Alfonso of Aragon (1448-95), Duke of Calabria, afterwards Alfonso II, King of Naples (1494-5), whose coat-of-arms appears on f.14.

f.297r. The Resurrection, with the Three Marys approaching the tomb. On the right is the Risen Christ holding a banner, and on the left appearing to Mary Magdalene in the garden. At the bottom of the page the smaller miniature shows the Harrowing of Hell.

Salting Collection no. 1224. MS. L. 2387-1910.

North Italian (Padua); *c.*1465-70.
Petrarch, *Sonetti, Canzoni e Trionfi*. Italic script in Italian.
23 × 14 cm. 187ff. Three frontispieces of coloured drawings, two on tinted vellum. Two illuminated pages containing the opening lines of the text of the *Sonetti* and *Trionfi* in coloured capital letters.
From comparison with other texts known to have been written by him, the scribe has been identified as Bartolomeo Sanvito (1435-after 1518). The frontispiece reproduced here from this fine humanist manuscript shows the influence of classical inscriptions and grave reliefs on the Paduan school of scribes and illuminators. Two artists appear to have been responsible for the illuminations, one of whom was probably Franco dei Russi.
f.9v. A tomb with the busts of a man and woman (interpreted as Petrarch with Laura, the woman who inspired him to write poetry), flanked by winged *genii* holding torches, the symbol of death. Below, on the left, is a figure in the classical style holding a lyre (either Orpheus or Apollo), on the bottom right a shield (probably a later addition), with the arms obliterated but ensigned with a cardinal's hat. (For this manuscript see Alexander J.J.G., 'A Manuscript of Petrarch's Rime e Trionfi', in *Victoria and Albert Museum Yearbook*, vol. 2, pp. 27-40).
MS. L.1347-1957.

pictorial effects within the reduced dimensions of a book is today regarded as marking the decline of illumination as a valid art form. Contemporaries held the opposite view. The Croat-born Giulio Clovio (1498-1578) was regarded as the Raphael or Michelangelo of book illumination with a genius for painting in the grandest manner on the smallest scale. In the Clovio style, though almost certainly not by him, is an unusual form of illumination, an altar card with a finely composed miniature of the Last Supper, painted *c.*1550 [plate 28].

Three isolated examples of illumination from other countries, two of a much later date, must conclude this survey. The frontispiece painted by Georg Beck of Augsburg in 1494-5 is a major example of late German illumination. At first glance, in the absence of text, it looks like a panel painting but on closer inspection a book connection is revealed in the donor group of two clerics in the foreground. Here a scribe (Leonard Wagner) is presenting the manuscript he has written to an abbot (Johann von Giltingen, of the abbey of Ss Ulrich and Afra in Augsburg). Two complete Psalters painted by Georg Beck at approximately the same date are known, one now at Munich, the other at Augsburg; this detached leaf is probably

27
Italian (Florence); 1540.
Book of Hours (Use of Rome), known as the Hours of Eleanora de Toledo. *Cancellaresca formata* script in Latin.

13 × 8.5 cm. 137ff. 10 large miniatures enclosed in rectangular borders divided into panels filled with cameos, Medici emblems and Renaissance ornament. On f.1v the manuscript is signed and dated 1540 by a scribe who calls himself Aloysius; his identity has not been established. The book was formerly owned by Eleanora de Toledo (d.1562), daughter of Don Pedro Alvarez de Toledo, Viceroy of Naples, who married Cosimo I (d.1574), later Grand Duke of Tuscany, in 1539. This book may have been a wedding gift since both Eleanora's and her husband's arms appear on f.2v.
f.69v. Flight into Egypt.
MS. L.1792-1953.

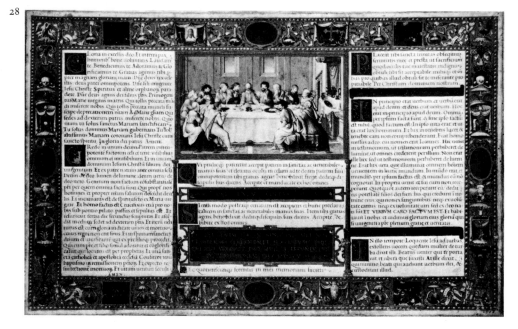

from a third. It shows Georg Beck to have been one of the most accomplished German book-painters in the late Gothic period [plate 29].

Spanish illumination in the fifteenth century was much influenced by the Flemish school but produced for the *cartas executorias de hidalguìa*, a category of manuscript peculiar to Spain though German examples are also known. These patents of nobility were produced in an unbroken sequence from the reigns of Ferdinand the Catholic and Isabella of Castille in the late fifteenth century right through into the nineteenth century. Before the King confirmed a grant of arms the petitioner was required to establish purity of blood from any Moorish, heretical or Jewish taint in himself and his ancestors, for which purpose many witnesses were called. Since few copies were required of *cartas executorias* their production was not a profitable field for printers but remained in the hands of scribes and illuminators. Though not always of the highest quality they are a peculiarly Spanish form of illumination. A considerable collection has been assembled by the V&A Library both as specimens of heraldic art and as examples of Spanish illumination in its later phases. Among the finest examples is the *carta executoria* in favour of the brothers Diego, Juan and Hernando de Almonte, of Seville, issued in 1626 [plate 30].

Our final example is also Spanish though written in Brussels. It is a *livre de piété*, written in Spanish by a scribe who signed himself Georg Herman Wilmart, a German-sounding name. He is known to have produced other devotional works, one dated 1658. The V&A manuscript testifies to the close, long-lived artistic relationship between Spain and Flanders. It is also a reminder that medieval illumination which began as an expression of religious faith and devotion was still serving this purpose in the Baroque age [plate 31].

It is usually asserted that the invention of printing from movable types in the 1450s killed the art of manuscript illumination. This is true only in the long term. The new technique had little immediate effect on the production of luxury manuscripts. Indeed, the most brilliant period of Italian Renaissance illumination and the spectacular development of the northern Ghent-Bruges school date from after, not before, the arrival of the 'ars nova'. Like most technological innovations, printing was at first viewed with reserve, if not disapproval, by bibliophiles, scholars, intellectuals, most of the clergy and members of the educated upper classes. Federigo Montefeltro, Duke of Urbino (ruled 1474-82), never allowed any printed books into his library of exquisitely written manuscripts.

Because the printed book was an entirely new phenomenon it took several decades before the appropriate forms in which it should appear became established. The early printers consciously strove to make their machine products resemble handwritten books as closely as possible, partly because they had no other model available and partly to reassure conservative clients who mistrusted anything new.

28
Italian; *c.*1540.
Altar card painted in the style of Giulio Clovio (1498-1578).
Roman script in Latin.
27.5 × 20 cm. The text is in three columns with a miniature of the Last Supper at the head of the centre column. The rectangular border contains scenes and instruments of the Passion together with Renaissance ornament. Altar cards contained portions of the Eucharistic prayers and were placed on altars to assist the memory of the priest celebrating Mass.
Dept. of Prints & Drawings.
MS. 2958.

Texts were often printed in double columns, as in manuscripts, initials left blank to be filled in and painted by hand, and woodcut illustrations coloured in imitation of miniatures. It was not until the mid-sixteenth century that printed books finally superseded manuscripts. Even today hand-written texts and illumination are still reserved for a few specific types of documents, rolls of honour, loyal addresses to the Sovereign, presentation scrolls to Lord Mayors and other prominent dignitaries, heraldic grants of arms and specially commissioned prayerbooks and marriage services. Apart from such official documents the medieval tradition is preserved and reinterpreted in a modern idiom in the work of members of the Society of Scribes and Illuminators (founded 1921). To give or to receive an illuminated book is an act which still confers a special lustre on donor and recipient alike.

29

29
German (Augsburg); 1494-5.
Detached frontispiece, painted by Georg Beck (d.1512), from a Choir Book written for the Abbey of Ss Ulrich and Afra at Augsburg.
40 × 28 cm.
The patrons of the monastery— St Ulrich, Bishop of Augsburg with a fish in his left hand and St Afra, clasping the tree to which she was bound at her martyrdom, are seated on raised benches. The hand of God extends from a cloud in the act of blessing. In the foreground Leonard Wagner, the scribe, presents his book to Johann von Giltingen, abbot of Ss Ulrich and Afra Abbey from 1482-95. Behind Wagner stands his patron saint, either St Jude or St Mathias, holding a halbert (attributes of both saints). Johann von Giltingen's arms appear at his feet. The attributed arms of St Ulrich (d.973), bishop of Augsburg who belonged to the Kyburg family, Counts of Dillingen, and of St Afra (d.303 during the Diocletian persecution of Christians) are introduced as part of the decoration of a late Gothic arch which also serves as a frame to the composition.
Dept. of Prints & Drawings.
D.86-1892.

44

30
Spanish (Granada); 1626.
Carta executoria de hidalguìa (patent of nobility) in
favour of the brothers Diego, Juan and Hernando de
Almonte of Seville. Granada, 9 May 1626.
This manuscript on silk is signed by the artist (a)
Jerónimo Rodriguez (1562-1640). The first frontispiece
(b) shows Hernando de Almonte and his wife kneeling,
wearing contemporary costume, before the Virgin
Mary who stands on a crescent moon surrounded by
angels and emblems (including the garden at her feet)
taken from the Litany of Loreto in honour of the
Virgin. In the frontispiece opposite (c) is the figure of
St James as *Santiago Matamores* (slayer of the moors)
on horseback.
MS. L.11-1981.

31
South Netherlandish (Brussels); 1673.
Memoria espiritual de devotas. Prayerbook written at
Brussels, signed and dated 1673 by Georg Herman
Wilmart. Roman script in Spanish.
11 × 5 cm. 68ff. Four miniatures and decorated
title-page.
G.H. Wilmart is known as a copyist of a Book of
Hours, dated Brussels 1658, and of other devotional
books (now in the Bibliothèque Nationale, Paris).
f.44v. Bust of the Virgin Mary within a pink
cartouche adorned with cherub-heads and standing on
claw feet. At her side a lily and a rod bearing leaves
(Aaron's rod?) with a crescent moon beneath, over
which is crawling a serpent with an apple in its mouth.
MS. A.L.1760-1894.

31

The Scope of the Collection

The examples of manuscript illumination in the V&A comprise both complete books and detached leaves or cuttings. They have been acquired to provide a corpus of examples illustrating one of the most important forms of medieval art and one of the most scintillating aspects of the art of the book. The collection makes no claim to be comprehensive or to represent all styles and periods of medieval book illustration. Nor can it be compared with the much larger and richer collections in the British Library, the Bibliothèque Nationale, in Paris, and the Vatican Library in Rome. Though much smaller in scope and number the Museum collection is, nonetheless, more than a heterogeneous assemblage of isolated examples. It includes several manuscripts and leaves of the highest quality and a larger number of more modest examples which cumulatively illustrate many aspects of the illuminator's art.

Oriental manuscripts, of which the Museum has a considerable collection, are outside the scope of this Introduction.

It is appropriate, in a museum of the decorative arts, that some manuscripts should have been acquired because they describe and illustrate one or more of the applied arts. The *Tre libri dell'arte del vasaio*, a copiously illustrated manual on the potter's art by Cipriano Piccolpasso (1524-79), was acquired as early as 1869, the splendidly illuminated Pliny *Historia Naturalis* in 1896. The latter contains a series of pictorial initials in Book xxxv illustrating various aspects of the painter's craft [plate 24].

In 1902-3 the collection was greatly enlarged by the bequest of 83 illuminated manuscripts from George Reid, of Dunfermline, Scotland. These came with the specific enjoiner that they should be available, under proper supervision, to students of illumination and lettering. During his lifetime Mr Reid had let it be known that it was for this reason that he intended leaving his manuscripts to the V&A rather than to the British Museum where access to manuscripts is restricted to accredited scholars.

Most of the Reid manuscripts are Books of Hours dating from the fourteenth and fifteenth centuries; late examples, that is, of the illuminator's art. With few exceptions they are not of the highest artistic quality, but it should be remembered that to study art history from only the best examples, the 'high spots', is to present an incomplete picture. Much may be learnt about the planning and execution of an illuminated manuscript from modest examples.

Since the Reid Bequest the collection has been considerably augmented. Later benefactors have included George Salting, whose collection of art objects of every kind is one of the finest bequests the Museum has ever received, David M. Currie and Sir Sydney Cockerell. Important purchases have also been made with the limited resources available for such costly items. These later acquisitions have been mainly in the field of calligraphic manuscripts. Important examples were acquired in the immediate post-war years by the Deputy Keeper of the Library, James Wardrop (d.1957), himself a distinguished expert on Italian humanistic calligraphy. Calligraphy and illumination overlap to a considerable extent but in this essay the emphasis has been on illumination.

Further Reading

Alexander J.J.G., *The Decorated Letter*, London, 1978.

Alexander J.J.G., *Italian Renaissance Illuminations*, London, 1977.

Avril François, *Manuscript Painting at the Court of France: the Fourteenth Century (1310-1380)*, London, 1978.

Backhouse Janet, *The Illuminated Manuscript*, Oxford, 1979.

Delaissé L.M.J., *A Century of Dutch Manuscript Illumination*, Berkeley (Cal.), 1968.

Harthan John, *Books of Hours and Their Owners*, London, 1977.

London: Victoria and Albert Museum, *Catalogue of Miniatures, Leaves, and Cuttings from Illuminated Manuscripts*, 2nd ed. London, 1923.

Meiss Millard, *French Painting in the Time of Jean de Berry: I. The Late Fourteenth Century and the Patronage of the Duke*, 2 vols, London, 1967, II. *The Boucicaut Master*, London, 1968, III. *The Limbourgs and their Contemporaries*, 2 vols, London, 1974.

Mütherich Florentine and Gaehde Joachim E., *Carolingian Painting*, London, 1977.

Narkiss Bezalel, *Hebrew Illuminated Manuscripts*, Jerusalem, 1969.

Nordenfalk Carl, *Celtic and Anglo-Saxon Painting: Book Illumination in the British Isles, 600-800*, London, 1977.

Panofsky Erwin, *Early Netherlandish Painting*, 2 vols, Cambridge (Mass.), 1953.

Randall Lilian M.C., *Images in the Margins of Gothic Manuscripts*, New York, 1966.

Réau Louis, *Histoire de la peinture au Môyen-Age: la Miniature*, Melun, 1946.

Rickert Margaret, *Painting in Britain: the Middle Ages*, 2nd ed, London, 1965.

Robb David M., *The Art of the Illuminated Manuscript*, London, 1973.

Thomas Marcel, *The Golden Age. Manuscript Painting at the Time of Jean, Duc de Berry*, London, 1979.

Weitzmann Kurt, *Studies in Classical and Byzantine Manuscript Illumination*, Chicago, 1971.

Weitzmann Kurt, *Late Antique and Early Christian Book Illumination*, London, 1977.

Wordsworth Christopher and Littlehales Henry, *The Early Service-Books of the Church*, London, 1904.

Note: The first three volumes of the important *Survey of Manuscripts Illuminated in the British Isles*, edited by J.J.G. Alexander, have appeared to date (1981). They are: I. Alexander J.J.G., *Insular Manuscripts 6th to the 9th Century*, London, 1978; II. Temple Elzbieta, *Anglo-Saxon Manuscripts, 900-1066*; III. Kauffman C.M., *Romanesque Manuscripts, 1066-1190*, London, 1975.